The Serpent's Rattle

A poetry memoir

Astrid Ferguson

Copyright © 2018 Author Name
Book Photograph © by Betsy Falco
All rights reserved.
ISBN: 1-7328669-0-2
ISBN-13: 978-1-7328669-0-4

DEDICATION

My siblings and everyone who has and continues to live in the middle of violent chaos.

TRIGGER WARNING

**This book
contains
sensitive material
relating to:**

**Child Abuse
Intimate Partner Abuse
Sexual Assault
Eating Disorders
Trauma
Violence
Attempted Murder
Attempted Suicide
& more.**

**Remember
to practice self-care
before, during & after
reading.**

CONTENTS

cAMOUFLAGE 4
vENOM faNgs 40
mOTIONLESS/ tHE breakDOWN 76
rESIDUAL effects 115
OVERcoming 138
aBOUT tHE aUTHOR 166

ACKNOWLEDGMENTS

My family. My closest friends. Everyone who read "MOLT" and requested to read more about my story. Last but not least, to you, reading these words right now. Thank you for releasing me from the serpent's cage.

Anywhere between 10-12 million people a year are physically abused by an intimate partner.

More than 20,000 calls are placed a day to domestic violence hotlines.

20% of women in the United States have been raped.

More than 1 in 3 women, 35.6%
more than 1 in 4 men, 28.5% in the United States alone, have experienced rape, physical violence and/or stalking by an intimate partner in their lifetime.

30-60% of perpetrators of intimate partner violence also abuse children in the household.

Facts based upon statistics from
The Nation's Leading Grassroots Voice on Domestic Violence and
The National Domestic Violence Hotline Statistics.

Astrid Ferguson

Hoja En Blanco

When the threading of these pages began, I would stare at the cursor asking it to say everything I couldn't. I was perplexed to tell another cliché, since telling the truth has become more of a cliché instead of a healing needle used to close open wounds. These pages are for all those locked diaries that burned tucked away under my pillow. These pages are for all the misspelled words, improper grammar, and bad attempted poetry formed from all the tears my bed absorbed. These pages are for the little girl who never asked to live in constant chaos. These pages are for all the whispers the universe never heard. These pages are for you sitting there wondering if the sun is real. These pages are for us who have lived with serpents. Who've felt left behind in prayer like a lost letter that never made it to Santa Claus. These pages hold every word the serpent hissed in venom for me to hold secret until my dying day. These pages are for the memories of who I once was, like a ghost from the future who has traveled the past in journals of ink – I told you we would make it.

-Astrid

Astrid Ferguson

cAMOUFLAGE

Serpents use tactics like blending in with their surroundings to appear invisible to the naked eye. A tactic often used for hunting prey. And that is exactly how this story begins...

The serpent appears like anyone else. They wear t-shirts, jeans, drive cars, work and smile as they wave a friendly 'hello'. They seem nice, trustworthy and conveniently appear in your life during moments of trauma, loneliness, and severe longing for affection. They create a character portraying the person you've been hoping for. They use white and blue brush strokes to paint themselves. Appearing more humane and persuasive while you grant them entry. Meanwhile, they keep their tails, fangs and their rattle of warning signals, hidden. Hypnotizing you into believing they're eagles with wings that can carry you into a safe haven of peace.

You see, all the stories begin the same way. At least, that was the tale I was told about the man in my house. The tale that always began with him helping during troublesome times. Oh, how serpents encompass what you lack during rock bottom; a way out. They appear to be guiding you into the light. They feed you lies disguised as truths, saying how they love you and how they make everything better.

Slowly, they disarm you. They convince your mind they are family. They convince your hands they are gentle and real. They convince your skin they are soft and tender. They convince your longing to halt.

The air begins to feel lighter, telling your lungs to work less, inhale. You can sleep once again.

This is how the serpent convinces you that it cares. Something you secretly haven't found within yourself, to care about loving yourself a little more than it's reptile deceit.

The Serpent's Rattle

She leaves beaches, warm sand, and palm trees,
for tall buildings, train stations, stairs and elevators.

In her dreams, she saw a big house,
shoes on her feet;
a car with all four wheels;
a job with her nameplate
outside her office near a penthouse suite.

Ecstatic by the perfect picture in this dreamlike ecstasy,
She tries to imagine the taste of the big apple.
Will it be bitter green or sweet red

In her dreams, however;
she knew exactly how to read maps.
She knew every bus,
she knew the driver's first name.
She knew the faces that gave up their seats.

Then her eyes opened wide,
this realistic dream seemed strange.
She doesn't understand anything;
she can't use her mother's native tongue.
Her neighbors won't offer her a plate of food.
The bodegas won't run a tab if she can't afford groceries.

She can't live with anyone;
no one accepts removal of weeds as exchange for rent.
She must live in a studio apartment,
share a room with a stranger;
this is everything that's affordable with her factory paycheck.

All of a sudden she finds herself working 10 to 12 hour shifts making barely enough to cover the cost of french-fries and a drink.

Her back hurts.
She gets sick.
She can't go to the hospital or request medical prescription because her job doesn't offer benefits.

She knows it's unjust,
but what can she do
No one understands her,
she can't afford a lawyer,
and
W H O   W OU LD   BE LI EVE   HER?

Desperation fills her soul to feed her children,
she goes hungry for days.
Fainting in sewing rooms,
stitching together dreams of the masters.
While she hangs from the needle in scorching hot solitude.

She does the only thing she can do,
the only thing that is free, even for her.
She prays this dream ends and awakens back home:
Santo Domingo.

She begs to hear the ocean again;
she insists on forgiveness for not dancing to the *gallos* song at 5 am.

Instead, every day she wakes up to another person asking
do you speak English
sew more pieces,
work overtime without pay.
It's a cycle that breaks anyone down,
making her feel comfortable staying,
hovered over,
bent in dismay.

-how the story of Implant mothers in America Unfolds

Dreams first form while sitting in the gaze of the unknown. It's a different beat. A different rhythm. An indescribable inkling that there is something beyond the horizon; something screaming 'hope'. Every immigrant starts this dreamlike journey when they look down at their feet and notice their shoes have holes. They look into their mother's eyes, bags full of sorrow, forming beds within their creases. They see the dirt on their hands and cars that pass them like ants in public parks. Something forms, a radical idea that there is a better life beyond the borders of home. Without exploring the danger, the vision expands, wings extend with the opening of eyelids, a new vision forms. A new struggle; a white washing of dirt from their hands and the R's from their tongues. Blending with the uniforms that dry clean rooms, sweat in factories, and a possible entrepreneurship in washing hair. The only dream allowed living within the steam.

A lesson learned: no matter how many bars of soap you use to erase your *accento*, your name and face don't match the description of the preferred resumé.

- how dreams are diminished to fit in pocket-size journals

The Serpent's Rattle

I like my hoops Big,
My ears wear them like proud signs – Latina.
I like to wear bracelets by the pack,
my wrist prefers them over the woven baskets
which my mother, and her mother, and her mother,
and the generations of mothers carried before me.

A mí me gusta mi arroz mojao,
Con habichuela y aguacate,
Con la ensalada en el mismo plato.

Yo cocino con salsa de tomate.
¡Aquí se come hasta las patas de gallina!

I like to wear long skirts with tropical colors,
So you can tell I'm foreign and remember
the women who worked the fields.

I like to wrap my hair in red, white and blue,
So you can understand my flags weren't worthy to carry star-spangled banners.

I like to gloss my full lips,
for I'm like the *limonsillos* that sweat in the sun.
First, you must bite into me *y lamber mi semilla*
Si quieres endulzar tu lengua.

I like to wear my hair in cuuurrvvess···
I pick its authenticity to increase the volume of creole
that broke French bondage.

I learned to speak the English tongue,
so I can tell my people:
immigration is a design to keep the lie expanding.
A lie that what was stolen and must be kept by denying us passage.

I'd like to invite my friends to sit at our table.
Let us discuss the wine we toast, made out of the blood and tears of
ourselves we call···
CHOCOLATE

-*this is Afro-Latina Fashion*
A new music invades from
the cracked opening
of the bared apartment window.
A familiar tune
gets louder as the trumpets sing;
the drums come in next
in cohesive harmony.
The lyrics form emotions in her head;
a rhythm takes over her body,
her hips imitate *la escoba.*
A new music invades
her ears.

A familiar tune;
rowdy voices,
a phrase all too familiar "*La Mega 97.9.*"
Subtle disagreements over baseball plays,
smells make homes out of her nostrils.
She can't look out the window,
her head is too big.

She decides to step out in her *bata*
roller set
(salons are not in the budget).
Looking like a sequel:
Grandma's on Sunday morning's sweeping front steps
She looks ahead,
it's coming from across the street.
It's
It's
It's

Una nueva bodega.

-nothing like corner stores to say 'hola mi gente' to people away from   *home*

Everything always begins on post-it's.
No strategy,
no plot or sense of organization.
But it begins… forming.
It's how the form turns into a questionnaire.

Dreams are like those notecards that you store in your treasure box.
Travel magazines with torn out pages;
the beginning of a foreigner's flight.
The flight before the visa envelops their welcome.

In our minds we paint picture maps,
scattered memos we store within ourselves.
They all begin with
'when I arrive I will live here'.
It's how the structure begins,
the structured beginning.

In our minds we see balconies,
children laughing,
bicycles with flowers.
The vision even includes a dining table with French toast, good American food.

Instead,
we blindfold our boney structure.
Hiding our hunger like beaded necklaces of frowns,
our dismantled chest,
and despair from our families.
Wearing our leg marks like stockings;
withstanding excruciating long hours on our feet.
It's when the reality sends a letter to our brain, titled
"The Beginning of Your American Story".

You simply don't learn to interpret hate.
You cannot phantom someone misleading you in a different language.
You forget there are no gardens where mangos can be plucked without an offering first.

You don't see the lonely,
the 'we are not the same'
imprinted behind low wages.
It's how survival of the fittest becomes your primary language.

First you sign here,
en inglés.

- *'post-it dreams', written in the wrong language, is how this story translates*

We grow like purple Hosta's
through the drought
in the shadows of our heritage.

We get divided when we
outgrow the pretty daisies.
Like implants, we get plucked
spread across appearing
Exodus watermarks.

Our children no longer bloom
in one place.
They change their color,
stems to green, so they can appeal to grass.

The mirage of growing
closer to the lawn.
Maybe, the landscaper won't separate us again.
Is this camouflage hope
or are these just
Wishful cries for unlearning visibility

-*Exodus Watermark*

Our stories included dancing in the rain.
Us twirling and laughing about
as days turned to nights,
and nights turned to days,
our ocean became a drought.
A dessert full of cacti.
We came wrapped in ribbons,
faces full of delight.
Discovering uncommon grounds.

Our parents implants.
Uprooted from the idea that adversity
taped shut our mouths.
They saw a great vision,
a possibility,
a perhaps; perhaps our clumsiness meant stumbling into
denied kingdoms with handed down crowns.

A forgotten truth
Peasants weren't allowed to cross the front yard
Our parents banned from opportunities
The checked boxes were marked 'temp files'
Opening positions for Consuelo's and Ramon's
Mechanics and maids, the only options to fill
Even the street signs read
Two ways
But it was clearly an alley way
where Caucasians tossed their trash on their way out.

So much rejection
beckoned the white dust to check-in nostrils
of familiar adults.
Following the town's wires on laundry days;
leading to faded smiles.
Batting dreams out of range.
Dining-room conversations
became stories of eviction notices to translate aloud.

-the stories of implanted children that grow up in between allies of lost identities

The summation of war and tragedy
Me

The result of love and hatred
Me

The composition of the in-between
Me

I am Latina-Dominicana and proud of it.
I am Haitian and proud of it.
I shouldn't have to choose between them,
Even if border lines divide them.

-so stop trying to make me choose which tongue to use to voice my orchestra

Astrid Ferguson

Friends will powder
Themselves in confetti sugar
While sticking their tongues in salt

-serpents hiding under drapes of skin

The Serpent's Rattle

I come from a town
Where rape and slavery comingled
Like a tossed salad,
Desperation voyaged us over
Like a canoe shaped leaf
Through the crocodile infested waters

The hope kept the stars sparkling
The only affordable lighting
Seeking refuge underneath
The same hands that demolished
Our originality

I don't know what is more spiteful:
Knowing that my home is just an infestation
Waiting to be quarantined
Or
Knowing that we were left this way
As a prediction, would we come begging
Again?

The arrival feels like a lioness
Whose leadership has been dominated

Astrid Ferguson

By lions she once charged with angst
Her uniqueness swept
She hides within trees
Waiting for the rivers to stream in smaller increments.

She awaits her chance
She flees
To an overthrown opportunity of change
If eyes are closed for a second too long
She will claim her reign··· again.

-Latinx   in   an   uphill   climb   to   leadership

The Serpent's Rattle

Lies grow like flies
    pestering the wind

Truth grows roots of stem
    wishing for wings

One with speed
    the other with wit

Who will outgrow who
    will depend
On compass readings
    your parents placed on your forehead

- the race to see which truth of embedded lies will grow first

Astrid Ferguson

I tell my story of transition
with a dialect too strong to mute – immigrant

You tell me your sorrows
linking chains of judgement – racism

Later we reach for knives
sharpened with affirmative action – employment

We divide our applications with stamps
light, dark, yellow, black, brown, and white – segregation

We recite manuscripts from Willie Lynch letters because it's a lesson that never loses excitement – persecution

We tell our children we love them
while we create lies of seasonal characters – programming

We converse just enough to keep our devils company – politics

Daily we do so much to keep ourselves disconnected to only glorify our imperfections – depression invitations

We constantly demand others to do things our way like we know all the answers—common policy

We judge the living but glorify the dead – abortion

We produce pentimenti of hood signs with perspective projects – gentrification

We keep our women in kitchens but question their baking measurements – glass ceilings

We raise our men as icebergs but demand emotional connection – sexism

We sign up for loans, electives and advanced classes just to receive rejection letters for not enough experience – broke(n) college graduates

Ironically, we don't demand experience to run for any of the three legislative branches – privileged applicants

We call this the land of the free, the land of the immigrants but yet you separate us and give us contaminated waters – unwanted residents

There was a time when we believed that
'united we stand and divided we fall'
was the mission of the American constitution.
Was it whited out when we found out
it was written by our brother,
the white man,
Or a privilege written in myrrh from every black women's stolen honey?

Since everyone is keeping score on their personal scoreboards;
consistently trying to one up each other,
I'll have a seat.
You let me know when we break even.

-left untitled so you can fill in which stanza you outscored

The Serpent's Rattle

Come back
    Come back
        Bright red roses with love as your fragrance

Come back
    Come back
        Elevation from this solitude
            Butterflies fluttering on the top of my stomach

Come back
    Come back
        Teach me how to grip you with the tips of my fingers
            Teach me how to cherish your voice
        Teach me how to make *habichuela con dulce*
        T e a c h   m e
            How to bend my knees and submit these imperfections
            In return for your affection

Come back
    Come back
        Teach me creole and how to make lamb soup

C o m e
C o m e
    B a c k
        Rewrite our story with sparkle and stardust
        Instead of a composed language that erased our humble beginning

-ancestors' story erased dialect

Failure supplements the sugar
she puts in her morning coffee
she stopped wishing for sunrise,
she doesn't care to cry all night.
As long as the next day the sun
didn't get to see the glow of her shame.

Her happy ending
Her fairytale story,
ended in three years,
with a 33 year division
and a little girl trophy.

As if her situation wasn't any worse,
after divorcing the only soul she knew in this town
she decided to take her little girl back home.
Only to find she was no longer there.

Her little girl's father stole their little girl as a rescue mission
And
Labeled her abandonment–
An oxymoron worth fighting the soldiers with wooden gavels with unsubstantial proof;
her foreign mother's milk
is as nutritious as the American formula.

Simultaneously, her daughter fights the good fight with demons of pneumonia and abusive caregivers.
She gives every last penny to the people in scrubs in white rooms.

The Serpent's Rattle

Leaving no money for lawyers,
for her voice to soprano equal representation.

And at that exact point,
The very bottom which the whiskey bottles reach;
The snake slithers in a chair next to her, and offers her a ride home,
in a language she could understand for the first time.

Hola, me llamo Simón.

-the custody battle that lured the Snake

I am not sure when the door cracked open. Maybe a locksmith gave out copies of our home key without our recollection. Whatever may have been the story, the serpent's entrance wasn't a forced entry. Court dates came following the feuds.

Airplane tickets to see who reached the promised land first became a race of who could parent best. Mother, due to hardships and lack of money, left me in Dominican Republic. Mother always said she would return for me.

An infuriated father showed up instead. Father said: "Who abandons their daughter?" Just as quickly as he said that sentence, I was taken from my grandmother. Returning to the statue of liberties and high rise buildings, I went. Except this time it was with my father, in a one bedroom studio.

I met my new babysitter, a strange lady. I saw the difference in her eyes. However, I was not one to speak since I had a large ball growing in my neck. It didn't allow me to say much except for *Thank you, ma'am.*

Sickness took hold of my body, shortly after being left to take naps in the cold floor with no warm clothes on. She would say it was my punishment for not eating when she instructed. Some great babysitter she was. The ball in my neck grew larger and filled with puss. My mother whom I did not get to see, and I couldn't tell her: "*I don't feel very good.*"

Daddy said: "*She doesn't have a court order to see me after her abandonment.*" The beginning of a battle between two parents while the battle for my life, my voice, began. Bronchitis and infections take over my home. Against the court order my mother rushes me to the hospital. Where I first meet the serpent. He was holding mom tight in his convincing hug of care. God, was it possible to meet two serpents in less than a week?

-serpents slither in through cracked doors while you sleep in despair

Sometimes we fail to see beauty in uncommon places.
Tell me the last time you breathed in the wind
and actually felt your lungs inhale an extra minute someone else lost?
Did you admire the eurythmic sirens
of knowing it wasn't you God chose that day?

The Serpent's Rattle

Tag was my favorite game
as a kid.
Tapping different shoulders,
so they can run and chase after you.

Now, as an adult,
I keep tapping each shoulder;
Like tag

YOU'RE IT!

- *adulthood   is   a   lonesome   place*

There was a time when women would get together. Conversing in honesty without malice or gossip. OK, forget that last part. Women always gossip. One of the major times where these conversations transpired, was during the salon. Now let me give you a Dominican salon's description, it can be any of the following:

- dingy cold basements
- sometimes a dining room
- a small area next to the kitchen
- a storage room
- sometimes a garage, not completely done but half *taller* (mechanic shop)

It was basically any place where we could have a sink and a *secadora* (hair dryer). Now during these conversations you will see some cooking going on, while the person is smoking a cigarette and doing your hair. There are no gloves involved unless you are getting your hair dyed, relaxed or something along those lines. So if a hair was found in the food, you'd simply remove it and continue eating. No big deal! There are no FDA regulations in Dominican salons.

Back to the conversations. When I used to live in New York, way back in the day, people called the land line. There were no text messages and you better hope the person had more than one line. If not, that line was always busy. However, among these conversations that transpired; one that was of particular popularity, *ella es un cuero*. My mother would say things like 'she wears a thong', *ella es un cuero*. 'She has a tattoo', *ella es un cuero*. 'She has a nose ring, a tongue ring, belly ring'. Any earrings that are not on your ears classified you as *cuero*.

The best one of all was when one of my mother's friends classified women as *cuero* for having a beeper in between their boobs (yes, remember beepers and two ways). Does that mean only men could carry and get paged on beepers? They usually clipped it on their belt. Did the location of the object matter?

The best debate of all used to be the one that went like this: 'man cheats on you, like many Dominicans do (don't fight me on this) he was just being a man'. If a woman did anything outside the religious aspect (mostly have made up), you were a *cuero*, a slut in the Dominican slang. So you didn't have to sleep around with different men to be considered a slut. You could just do un-lady-like Dominican classified things and that stapled you as *cuero*. Within that moment I thought to myself that if being like my mom: cooking, cleaning, never going out with friends, never doing her own thing, not working, not having a beeper, and not getting to speak her mind, meant she was *una buena mujer*, then I was going to be a *cuero*.

Sueños II (Dreams 2)

I should've known better
I should've carried a watch
I should've set an alarm.

Instead,

I let you take hold of time
I allowed you to create scenarios
Shower me in your pixie dust.

I should've known better
I should've learned sooner
I should've smashed your snooze.

Instead,

I allowed you to continue this foul play
With ballerinas, tutus and canneries singing
Operas
Melodies
And Sonnets that stuck in my head.

The most annoying ring:
wind chime,

to condemn me with your arrival tune.

Something, something,
something amazing is coming
Your perfect evil lie,
that a bright future awaits in a city where a woman holding a torch will set my opportunities a blaze.

- *you were the perfect lie my eyes couldn't unveil (reality)*

I come from a long line of peasants
Their struggles are written on my face.
I'm the result of homage,
Raped Slaves,
Colonized Tainos and
The paving of words we survived
Are carved in every wave of my curly hair

I am both the miracle and tragedy
Of two rivals separated by long lines of war
The love triangle of French versus the Spanish
The butter pecan shaded in between
Too dark for England
Too light for Africa
A child who was born into dual citizenship

A 53 year old Haitian father, turned American
A 20 year old Dominican mother
A creation of old versus new

I guess that makes me more American than foreign
A citizen born abroad
A certificate worth more than a Grammy

All these accolades
But not a single one saved me from oppression
From my own kind

Because I was still born, girl.

-the history of mankind

Astrid Ferguson

vENOM faNgs

Él la abre como una Yuca
He splits her open like a Yuca
Making breakfast out of her
Setting her limbs a float
Like poached eggs

Frying her impurities
Making a garden out of her womb
Erasing her father's legend with gentle kisses
whispering promises; *your heart is safe with me*

She allowed him to convince her senses
Down to a snoozed breeze
With reality turned off
She tuned into the resonance of his breathing

He allows her to stay
Entangling her mind like a yarn of
Want and need
She needs to want
A wanting need

It is within this very moment
When she hears the crickets in pitch black

Say, *you forgot to ask one very important question*
If he makes breakfast out of you
Will he make dinner out of his wife once he leaves
It's a detail she over sought

Because he became a thing: a boiling need.

-boiling yucca at 5 am

The Serpent's Rattle

Once the dust settled, things became quiet and strangely serene
Like any snake in a dessert who likes to keep their prey
feeling comfortably.

That is exactly when the first tactic uniformed,
this serpent decided to use tactics
masters used on their slaves.

    Segregate   Isolate
Causing a confusion of the brain;
in comfort at the grace of its tail.

It breathed in her every move of hers while she thought it was
a friendly hug.
It began to learn things about her that she had yet to self-
educate about.
This is how happiness began for little girls who lived with
snakes.
They never believed they were in danger
their mothers never shouted
R U N   R U N   R U N

Astrid Ferguson

Girls simply learned to follow orders like 'good girls',
Just like mama would declare.

- happiness in a comfortably scary place

The Serpent's Rattle

Mornings always began the same
sometimes, the sun shined,
sometimes, it didn't.
The order in which events occurred was always a given,
It was the unwritten rule.

The oldest sibling wakes up first.
Brushes their teeth,
Takes a shower,
Combs their hair,
Eats breakfast and prepares for the walk to school.

It was expected to check on the younger children
It's what big sisters did,
But since momma was home
She did all the mending.

Until my sister was of age for kindergarten,
It became my duty to walk her to school
And make sure she reached her classroom.

Astrid Ferguson

She became my shadow
and I, I became
her guardian angel.
Just two sisters walking, skipping
Through the gloomy park of Harlem
Full of empty syringes
On their way to school.

Then one morning everything changed.
I remember the rain trickling,
A thunderstorm caused the medal bars to tap the window.
Unsure if it was the wind, the rain, or the thunderstorm.

The shouting got louder,
The screams entered the door
Just like a scene in a horror movie.
Momma and the serpent had been arguing all morning over taking us to school.

Instantly I wake up from my bunk bed,

The Serpent's Rattle

Just not fast enough
Before···
He lifts her like a light keg of beer by her t-shirt
And she goes flying across our dresser
Hitting the TV, toys, and so much more.

She begins to bleed,
She tries to hide the embarrassment,
by telling us to stay in bed

He leaves without apologizing,
I knew then what the serpent's rattle sounded like on a rainy day.

- *the first song I heard with the serpent's rattle*

Funny how chaos
Feeds order

Order feeds chaos
Chaos feeds order

Order feeds chaos
Chaos feeds order

CHAOTIC
ORDER
CHAOTIC
~~Order~~ disorder

A never ending cycle of who will win at the end of every round.

Ding!

- Taoist's symbol of who's more masculine in slithering silence

The Serpent's Rattle

Bones crushing
as they pierce
through her flesh.
Pain in her heart
grows heavier
than a thousand
pounds of gold.

Knees buckled, giving in to gravity
Her feet have forgotten to hold her stance.

Her appearance resembles dead cattle
Hanging from a cliff alongside a main road,
Her face a chipping billboard with red and blue marks;
She has shattered into a million pieces of shard.

Her windows no longer condense light.
Hidden behind a mask of iron and wrapped in a black cloak,
She walks unbeknownst to pavements, like a zombie–
Monday to Friday, morning and night,
Smiling on the outside,
While the taste of black thickens inside.

She has become so used to the pain,
She no longer raises her hands to prevent,
Or steps out of the way from
Blows of concrete by human hands.

She stops breathing;
She stops believing;

Astrid Ferguson

She stops fighting;
She stops loving the idea of a better tomorrow.
Today she just remains the victim in a censored face.

-abuse is the most intelligent villain hunting prey

The Serpent's Rattle

A composite truth
A comfortable storm
A soft black night
Darker is warm

The black bird croaks
A witchcraft hunt
All things little girls fear
Except for one

She befriends
The red moon
So the sun could never reveal
The black and blue(s)
Under her scarf

A beginning,
A girl's tale turned woman.
The conversations of sanitary napkins,
The protection,
The child bearing.

A middle ground of what to expect,
The cramps
The Midol dosages
The *botiqin* of pain relievers

Tampons
Good girls don't wear them
Unless you're sexually active
Tú estás teniendo sexo
Was that a statement or momma's way
Of asking if I knew how boys felt?

A plot twist
The porn tapes
The serpent's tongue on my clitoris,
Enforcing hammer head into my mouth,
Circling unwanted hands on my immature areolas.
He said it was 1 on 1 lessons

An upside down ending
A filled tub

The Serpent's Rattle

Flooded with a whales bellies worth of water and soap
To wash away the shame.

The unsaid words.
The untold event.

The 'No's' whispered in nostalgia left unheard.

The scared light push.

Is it more cynical to own a found gold mine
Between your legs
Or sit on a treasure you wish was never yours — sheet stains

- how many bars of soap does it take to wash away a serpent's hiss

Astrid Ferguson

I said no in my head
I said no with my hands
I said no in every way without using my words

Did he think it was OK to still touch me
Did he think it was OK for a 35 years old man to feel attracted to an eleven year old

How did he think in his mind this scene would play out
Did he think it wouldn't crush me
I know he didn't think at all
That was the problem

He was just thinking of his physical needs
He didn't think I was his daughter too
At least that's what Momma wanted me to believe
I guess when you're not related by blood
It makes these things OK

I kept my mouth shut;
Not to protect him
But to save myself from saying,
I screamed 'No' and was afraid,
Momma forgave him the next day
The same way she forgave him every time

he punched her in the face.

-*The only regret that still haunts my bed*

No phone call
No phone call
No voicemails
No voicemails
No charges of stealing
No charges of stealing
Change out of dresser draws for candy.
Change out of dresser draws for candy.

No phone call
No phone call
No voicemails
No voicemails
No charges of stealing
No charges of stealing
Belt with pointy studs
Belt with pointy studs

Kitchen stove burner turned on high flames
Kitchen stove burner turned on high flames
Fingertips begin to dissipate
Fingertips begin to burn
Skin hardens
Skin peels off
Momma just watches the serpent's game of who's in charge of the change in the drawer.

- *child abuse left unseen was my sentence for taking one dollar in change out of his chest drawer*

Do you know where fires begin?

    They start
    In your brain
    Spread like wild flowers
    Throughout your body called /).(\

– RAGE

I hated the way you followed him
Around
Like a mouse without a colony.

I hate the way you accepted
His words like some
Unwritten policy

I hated how you continued to sleep
In the same bed as him
Knowing he watched my showerhead
Knowing
    Knowing
        Knowing

He touched me
He stalked me
He hit me
All while he was supposed to be working

I hated
    Hated
        H A T E D
The way you broke into a million pieces
Every time you warned to leave

You died inside
An empty soul lived behind your eyes
Frailty and osteoporosis filled,
Occupying your physicality

Somehow your tongue still kept a burning flame
A conviction for not doing chores right
Something your children had to pay

Teachers would ask me to define role models
I couldn't think of a single one
I only had the perfect example
Of whom I wouldn't become
I hated
    Hated
        H A T E D
This boiling lava oozing to reach a river of pasteurized hate

How could he hit you
Smack you around
As if you had flies on your face

Throw you against drywall
Step on you like concrete
Beneath his feet

How could you tolerate this
How could you sacrifice me and leave me with no bullet proof vest

He would call you crazy
It was his favorite line of judgement
When his fangs needed to replenish its venom

I hated begging
Asking
Pleading you
To leave
While your response was
Always consistent
Little girls shouldn't get in adults business

I hated
    Hated
        H A T E D
The collection of bruises on your face
The pouring outrage
Of your cries due to his unwarned penetration – ongoing rape

Your legs running
Your hair breaking from the pulling
The stress
The miscarriages

I hated
    Hated
        H A T E D

The Serpent's Rattle

How dismantled you became
Believing this lifestyle was normal
I guess that is what happens when your friends accept the same
I hated how you tried convincing me this was love
As if bunnies could live in cages with anacondas
And live to tell the next day

I tried keeping these words a secret
These feelings dug in a pit
Allowing their demons to spread toxins around my voice
Keeping me silent in bitterness
Every time you forced me to call him father
When you both weren't worth my acknowledgement.

Treating me like Cinderella,
An unpaid sitter,
 A free translator;

I hated
    Hated
        H A T E D
Caring about you so much
I hated calling you a relative.

-how little girls build walls around things that are not okay

I used to sit in the back of the classrooms.
I avoided participating at all cost.
I wouldn't raise my hand even if I knew the answer;
skirted any chance to speak.
I didn't want to hear the laughs for pronouncing anything incorrectly.

As many laughed in revelry,
Simply for repeating my guardians syllables.
I was safer in silence
I was accepted within my swollen throat.
I was unnoticed in the back.
In solitude, I handed fear for the gold medal;
It owned the most important muscle I stopped exercising.

-Self-advocacy

The Serpent's Rattle

Little girl,
Learn how to swallow pain like Tylenol.
Take it with a tall glass of your saliva.
Clench your teeth shut and swallow your tongue.

Little girl,
Learn to accept glass stillettos weren't created in your size.
Wrap your feet to keep them from outgrowing old shoes.
Just like momma crazy glues your sneakers like crazy,
We have a broken image to upkeep.

Little girl
Learn to accept the devil in your bedroom and dance to the rattling of serpent's music.
Pick your poison–
Bachata, salsa or merengue

Little girl,
Learn to reverse fear into comfort,
Comfort into a numb version of boiling rage
Transpire them within the margins of notebook pages.
Trust me, no one listens to the fragility of women, screaming 'rape'.

Little girl,
Learn the advanced mathematics,
So you can calculate how many
meals you'll force down your throat before
your beauty inconsideration comes to a halt.
Bring an end to this constant need
For society's hug,
and begin accepting your frame as an outlier to a pretty woman's hub.

Little girl,
Count, count, count once more the countless ways you pray,
For your mother to leave her oppressor
But it only seems like God doesn't give you much fame.

Little girl,
Accept the serpent is now the father of your siblings,
Give his hands a pass
He's not going anywhere
Even if he takes off his mask.

Set the table
Remember where the spoon goes
These good table etiquettes will come in handy
When you serve a better financial status

Little girl,
This story doesn't have a happy ending,
You're not a princess,
You're not even the evil step-mother.
You're the step child, Cinderella,
That never makes the ballroom or has a fairy godmother.
Little girl, little girl
Learn that life is about taking this pain cold,
Crochet your own crucifix.
There are no knights that come to rescue peasants,
Not even in the movies,
No matter how loud they scream.

Little girl, pay attention:
Do you see that shiny object?
It's waiting to fill your conscious
Before you decide to point it straight to your temple
Remember selfishness is also the devil
This is a real nightmare but you still can
open your eyes and listen

Little girl··· *somos iguales*
You are me.
Wait a little longer
For life begins
When.
You.
Stop.

Crying
For
Equality.

Imagine a world without
Rosa Parks, Harriett Tubman, feminism, Elanor Roosevelt, or women marches.
As little girls we'd still be sitting with our legs crossed instead of rewriting history so our little girls can believe in dreams

Little girls are more than the flour they used to bake, they are more than the diamond she holds between her legs

-a message to you little girls, dream wildly instead of growing comfortable sitting within a naysayers space.

The Serpent's Rattle

Sundays were made for church
A day to sit on hard wooden benches
Prayers and kneeling on pews
Praising the sermons
Repenting for sins of impurity
Comparison to Virgin Mary

Always wondered if church was like sunlight that burned vampires
For no matter momma's efforts
The serpent never came past the front door
A silent prayer conjured in my head

If I steal this holy water
and use it to poison the serpent
while reciting our father
will I be forgiven for my sins

Then came time for the holy wafer
To slip down my throat
A fantasy of an arc forming around mother
embarking her to found strength
Protection from his venom
A repeated prayer

Maybe that is why he convinced her to never confess; so the wafers would never crumble inside our bodies to deliver us all···

-when you place hope in catholic wafers that never break bread
(Prayer   1)

Interpreting the Bible like a tainted vernacular
Praying for the benediction
While kneeling waist deep in wrath temptation

Maybe, the bread wasn't a doxology
Instead,
It was Satan's white flour sprouting like carbs of obesity in a skinny cup

How many times must I pray only to return to a snakes den
(the universe never responded)
It's how fairytales end and reality sets in
No one will save us because we're not worth their savings

-the moment hope ends and hate begins (Prayer 2)

"Be still," God says
"Be still in silence···"

In this silence
A reverse metamorphosis occured
I became a butterfly with wings full of bullet holes
I decided since I was told to sit
Why continue to attempt trying to fly

Locating sunrooms just to feel grace again

I decided to follow orders for once
I traded in my broken wings for a carved stone
I became a boulder
My veins, winter
My hair turned fall
Only to keep my eyes warm

Following every detail in the ripples left by flying leaves
The astrology became clear
Serpents can't bite through stone

- when scriptures are carved in stone (Prayer 3)

She is angelic with wings of red paint
She wonders if he sees her honesty and feels a beating heart
She hears his loud breathing as he devours her flesh
She saw herself in perfect T-shape among the shadows of sin
I want to feel loved but I settle for his lies instead

She grows shame as allowance from the crucifixion he assembled to feed his thirst
She pretends to collapse in the dishonesty of his spine
I feel like torn pages of spilled ink within secret diaries

She touches her palms to feel the nails he dug in her skin
She worries the transition of his dishonesty will fill a uterus with nine months of what if's
She cries but yet still loves his name
I still get excited by the idea of carrying your last name

She understands this is a battle in which his war will win
She agrees to stay even after knowing she dies a little more under the moons forgiveness
She dreams of one day digging, finding, removing each fang he planted in her skin
I try to stand instead of leaning like a plate on a placemat in open space

She hopes one day her savior will shed light
Before her eyes become so blinded by the wounds that fertilize rage
She's still there,

The Serpent's Rattle

Trying to learn how to exhale the love he never gave

– it's how the serpent constricts you (victim) in an illusion that this pain and suffering is love he injected in your veins

A brewing storm
A cracked window
An attempted break-in
A defused bad decision
An opened door
A subtle last conversation
In the basement where scarecrows tell
A just in case he tries his physical brawl tactics
A metal object tucked away for protection: knife

Have you ever been afraid,
So afraid, you're willing to fight until the end.
Even if it becomes an archived murder case?

The dispute leads to a wrestling match
A choked neck,
Yanked hair from her scalp
With intoxication fogging his perception
She reaches
She inserts
She wins the fight

Blood spills over the floor like a river of revenge
Lights fill the hallways
The little faces sleep soundly
Unaware of their mother's plea for self-defense

The Serpent's Rattle

She's taken in handcuffs
She's been assaulted once before by the same man
Apparently, he's assaulted women in three other states,
But, that doesn't justify the bloody knife

That what the policemen said

Within this plot twisting night,
She learns, she will give birth to this dead man's son,
Unaware of the harm she caused (boyfriend's/baby father's death)
Orange becomes her new black wardrobe,
The doom's door welcomes her home
She is charged with murder
of the father of her unborn son.

She gives life to a dead man's son (behind prison doors)
She stares into the face of a boy who will call her 'mom' and 'daddy's murderer'.

How do you explain; I love you but I'm a felon for sending your dad home for self-defense,
Saving us meant killing him.
I guess that's what happens when you don't let him break in
You let him come in through the front the door, drunk.

Now we have to live, hating to love each other
You and I
My son

-giving life and death inside rib cages of a black woman's self-defense (Natalie)

Blank___
>   It's a familiar state

Blank ___
>   It's a common emotion, uncontrollable feeling

Blank ___
>   It's how awkward conversations begin

Blank ___
>   Creates the illusion that you need fill-ins

Blank ___
>   Is the ambiance created when you start to believe life is your tyrannical permanent residence

Blank ___
>   Is what you accept in exchange for isolation from the universe's shame

-dwelling in draft mode after the serpent steals our name

Astrid Ferguson

mOTIONLESS/tHE breakDOWN

The Serpent's Rattle

Home is supposed to be the place
where the heart feels safe.
The mind rest in tranquility;
The body relaxes from physical agony.
Your feet levels to meet your knees,
While watching TV screens.

It is the place where you can rest and recover
You laugh uncontrollably,
You invent and bring your thoughts into vivid creativity.

At least that's what I've been told
It's the stories my friends would share
When I was asked
What about home did I like most
My mind went blank.

See I didn't share the same experience
Home was the one place I dreaded most
I would walk the longest routes home
To prolong hell a little more

I lived with Satan,

Damion and Judas,
Wrapped in a fucking bow tie

The days depended on his moods.
Maybe if he had enough angel dust,
Watched enough porn,
Earned a few more bands from the poison he sold,
He would let us enjoy a good night's rest.

I didn't know how to tell people,
Maybe if he fucked mom hard enough and made her forget about her broken nose,
His hands wouldn't find their way to my bunk bed.
I just didn't know how to say,
I hated them both,
I hate my home.

-the place I called home

The Serpent's Rattle

When momma was naked
She asked me
Run your fingers down my collarbone
Tell me if you can feel my wings

I replied, *I'm sorry.*
All I feel are scars
Can wings regrow

With her head bowed down
She responded:
I gave it to the serpent
He convinced me
My body was not my own

So we remain at the tail end of the soaking tub
Trapped.
Her in purgatory,
I in sinful thought.
Deciphering if electrocution
Would stop the venom
From spreading
To our silent beating
Hearts.

-a conscious decision to give up freewill

Astrid Ferguson

To take a good picture
You must fill-in all holes

To plant gardens in the minds of strangers
You must evenly s p a c e seeds of growth

To seal in your windows and doors
You must fill all around with foam

So much time is spent f i l l i n g   i n
Little is left f e e l i n g the soul

That is the empty hole
Serpent's nestle,
Hibernate,
Until it swallows you whole.

- *filling in*

Everyone can see it
The purples
The blues
The black

Everyone can see it
The tears
The fear
The pleas

Everyone can see it
The cycle
The invasion
The death
The forgiveness

Everyone can see it except for me.

-the silent thoughts of being ashamed to run but enduring the stay (domestic abuse victim thoughts)

What is simple
If not an over saturated thought
That respect is given
That love is cherished
That life is protected
That you will treat me like I treat you,
With immense kindness.

What is simple
If not an overly complicated algorithm
That men shouldn't beat girls
That girls should be submissive to their men
That women are our Mother Earth and men our sunshine.

What is simple
About you and me
That every time perpetrators raise their hands,
They attack the children next.
That abuse is like that Kool-Aide packed with diabetes
Everyone drinks from its well
That quenches irrational voices–
An echo's inheritance.

What is simple
If not a secret that our mothers never tell
Our fathers a prediction of treachery sins,

Adultery before loyalty

What is simple
About love anymore if we still hide
From thoughts of loving ourselves
More than we love loving the romance of pain

-the irrational makes simple too complicated so it makes loving serpents deceit easier until the implausible expires the victim's stay (life or death)

Sexual assault is the language everyone
Stutters to speak
Falls on deaf ears
and
Braves its way into the caring mute
That can't help remove the assaulted bolt.

-reason why so many don't report, our reports are never marked with hope

The Serpent's Rattle

Saying I was raped
Ten,
Twenty
Years later,
Means
You reached a statute of limitations on your respect

Saying he raped me
The same day
It happened
Questions of who provoked who
Emerge like bees protecting their hives

No one asks how can we help you
Repair
What was stolen from you

-it's never a good time to report indiscretions

Astrid Ferguson

Subconscious is a location
where reality and fallacy
hurt each other.

Subconscious is a secret chamber
entrance to malignant seesaws,
that outweigh what the eyes see and
what the mind dissects.

Subconscious is a permanent guest
sitting in the attic
yelling down
use the spiral staircase.

Subconscious is where you first learn
that you are in danger,
but your limbs become frozen
turned to frost, a hopeless daze.

Subconscious is the same corner
she sits in front of the mirror,
broken
holding her knees tightly against her cheeks
soaked in the shame of imprisonment.

A deeply rooted love
for a son of God.
Whom breaks her down like a Rubik's cube;
To break and solve just as easily

as he says,
I'm sorry and I love you.

-subconscious is the place between reality and fallacy that every victim turns to a prisoner of stay in intimate partner domestic abuse

Words can be used like arrows
Spinning to leave a permanent
Lasting impression – Scars

Words can demolish empires
With strong letters and syllables
Filter incoherence through communities
Infect ear drums
And foster an epidemic sickness in our minds

- verbal abuse is the first form of synthetic depression

When did we
become volunteers in jail
When did we
decide to promote ourselves as caged birds
When did we
Let guards stand by the front door that remains open
When did we
Become so fragile to strength
When was the turning point
    The time when we missed our exit
    We missed the left turn

    Actually, stop at the octagon
    Rushed instead of proceeding with caution
        Through
            Through
                Through
                    Ourselves

- when did we become abusers and victims of our flesh

First they pierce you with words
Then
They band-aid you with rejection
After
They drown you in the alcohol of irrelevance
And gauge you with hate
While you hold your breath
And mouthwash your oppression
And spit out air bubbles of faith

-the constant spring cleaning of pleading acceptance

The Serpent's Rattle

a time arrives / the clock dings a dong / prayer can't save you
the phone takes too long / you can scream at the top of your lungs
no one / no one / not one / will respond

fear strikes first / violence swings a loud hung / death hits a flat
note / who will instrument the home run

will it be the batter / another woman beaten like a runaway slave
or / a dead man killed in a brawl trying to make it to second base /
the skin drums are roaring / a choice will come

a short breath / a silent hum / someone / someone someone / breaks
down the door / who leaves in handcuffs / who will the chalk draw
as the dead outcome

all questions left unanswered / by the justice system / a violent act
can be forgiven if it's a man holding the gun / it's called standing
your ground / not self-defense / another woman won't be saved
from the doom doors coffin / here she comes / another inmate
plotted revenge / the prosecutor secured the charges

the unpredictable hour / a minute too long / a second too late / went from an exhausted survivor / to a murderer, an unforgettable consequence / the ending of domestic violence / attached to cases left unsolved behind the secretaries complaint cabinet

children are left unprotected to run into another serpent's cousin.

-self-defense results in a woman's cage for a man's free gain

He damages her outer layer
Dressing her limbs in welts
Bringing her down to pick her teeth like razor blades
Tempting her to bite off her own flesh
Force feeding
I'm weak and ugly in every way
As a replacement meal plan
In between the smacks and rape

She reaches rock bottom
Deciphering how to begin feeling again
Pinning proper reactions on story boards
While leaving her self-worth in the dirty laundry basket
Wearing chaos as her society assigned figure dress

Imagine if every woman fought back every:
Rapist / abuser / harassment / black mailer / human trafficker / boyfriend / friend / husband / uncle / cousin / brother / stranger
That soiled her name
How flooded do you think the prisons would get
How often would you blow past your newsfeed because it would become too repetitive
You wanted entertainment instead of this again

-*women this is your permission to be selfish without regret*

I come from a view where the cable lines divides the sky
> The bricks are shaded maroon, burgundy and grey disguise.
> The molding is black,
> A villain of pure.

I come from a view where the cable lines divides the sky
> A place where the perfect black boxes are separated by medal prisons.
> A norm where potatoes are mashed for breakfast.
> The pools flew from fire hydrants
> To cool our legs from the elevator-less apartment complexes.

I come from a view where the cable lines divides the sky
> Where dividing meant sharing the small riches of cigarette butts we found, because that is all the high we could justify.

> This view where wishes extend from cornrows,
> Places with fans that blew hot air on hot summer days.
> See, AC was for the rich folks,
> Still, we cook *Sancocho con arroz*
> As if we weren't dying from a heat stroke.

I come from a view where the cable lines divides the sky
> It's like the Lord's way of saying *you got a long way to the beach*

The Serpent's Rattle

In here they serve ignorance for sand,
Hatred for palm trees,
And a mean fist for breakfast.

A place where sidewalks became memoirs with cheap roses and prayer candles for those who were violently killed.
I wouldn't know the full stories because in our town that was called snitching.

I come from a view where...
>They tell you to fear the white man but it's my kind sleeping next door that keeps molesting me.
>Trying to force me to suck his dick,
>Beating down mother because she chose to wear a sheer shirt one day.

I come from a view where the cable lines divides the sky
>A place where you learn about coke
>Because you get accused of stealing drugs you had no idea was being cooked in your room in the first place.

I come from a view where the cable lines divides the sky
    A forsaken place where screams were your alarm for saying *you didn't escape this shit today.*
Bruises, black eyes, rape were just parts of an average day.
Since momma wore them like accessories on her face,
I guess they were just like earrings that clicked right into place.

My view of the sky would get foggier by social aspects; news of violence taking my friends.
We never communicate support like syrups on pancakes.
English being my second language and my Spanish friends making fun of my poor image.
It's a place where no one bothers to give you a compliment.
No one sees you moving out of the fifth floor unless you're evicted.

An address where food stamps are bonus checks.
They get sold for cash so we can afford new nails and Jordan's.
I know,
I see it now when it comes out every paycheck.

I come from nothing except cable lines that never powered a good day.
> Until, I decided to cut them down ,
> so you can look at my sky,
> Face to face.
> See the sunrise and the sunset.

> So go ahead;
> Tell me. I'm worthless, without using the moon eclipse as your fucking sidekick.

> I'll tell you,

I came from a view where the cable lines divided the sky,
> But today I'm holding the mic telling you
> I found a new cable line that allowed me to survive every challenge, without any man present.

Too busy living in your head
Dying of drought
Too much sunlight burns the leaves

-too busy dying to live outside the brain

The Serpent's Rattle

They say you can't run out of words
But you can run out of ink.
Find your own typewriter.
I've been fucked up for too long
I don't even know where to begin.

Just this once allow me to weep in the sorrow
Of just not being OK.
I beg you to just stop plaguing me with your humanity.
Stop saying you care but calling my story a cliché.

-tired of writing how to heal, ink can't make us change

Astrid Ferguson

Long walks held my secret tears
in their afternoon breeze.

Stoop steps kept my bruised legs, safe.

The concrete concealed my hatred of returning home.

The weeds grew from the long tears I wept,
I wept
    I wept
        I   w e p t
By every park filled with empty syringes of heroin.

Rage began to BOIL
An i n a b i l i t y   to understand
Hemotoxic manifesting in momma's veins.

A wall formed
A mother no longer to be had
A best friend buried in soils of dead grass

I have come into this world alone
I have been abandoned
Without being left in a basket before church doors

The Serpent's Rattle

I became strong for me
No longer caring for the womb that carried me.
You may find that cruel,
Some may say psychotic,
But in this chaos something brewed
To the top of my teacup's brim,
Love couldn't grow where the shadow's fog hung.

First, I hid my bruises with cream.
Father was too old to fight off the serpent.
I was strong enough,
Just enough.
To hide from the world
To numb the pain
Becoming emotionless

Just like a blank page.
(*everyone filling margins with their own insane*)

- *life within a fourteen year cocoon of the serpent's cage*

The broken dishes she throws at him out of fear
Desperation
The sheets that holds her secrets of continuous rape, comforters (comforting her)
The phone calls she has in secret with all the friends that take punches just like her
The hotlines she calls 100 times a day
To hang up shortly after hearing "Hi, can I help you?"

The kids that watch her enforce her solitary confinement from all social transparency
The bottle
The open hand
The closed fist
The corner sofa
The knuckle valleys of blood
The silence behind the idea of loaded gun clips;
He used
To hit
Her
Condemning her further into misery

Somehow,
Between the gaps of her welts

She must factor in your manly reputation

-the programming of living in silence

Who screams louder
The cold floors that breaks our falls
The table that pretends to catch us mid-air
Later dropping us like a bad joke
With broken legs

The police reports that hide behind
Filing cabinets and hanger files
No charges
The common history of domestic violence
Alex Marissa warning shots resulting in twenty years of self-defense agony
Behind prison bars
No murder committed yet
She was considered a danger to society

-another woman behind bars for exercising self-defense

Astrid Ferguson

To make *pasteles*
You have to set aside fifteen hours
Of boiling
Smashing
Folding
Seasoning
To freeze overnight folded in green leaves

They say *pasteles* get better over time
The longer they freeze
The more you have to boil to make them soft,
Enough to eat in just a few bites.

I like to think of the women in my family like the *pasteles*
We've spent so much time *cosechando*
That our beauties froze under the mashed plantains
Tostones y mofongo

We are not just beautiful in the kitchen
We're beautiful intellectually.

So today ask us to be your guest
Show us that we deserve
A good meal without asking for *el pilón,*
You should smash your own garlic for once.

-Dominicanas can be served too

They can take your voice
They can take your mind
They can own your thoughts
They can turn fear into your only choice
They can push away the chair so you can fall into a handicapped state

They can
take and take and take
And they will keep taking until you have nothing else to give

What is left,
YOUR   SOUL.
They would take that too,
Except it isn't yours to give.

When will you start taking instead of giving what is rightfully yours

-stop   accepting   withdraws   and   start   looking   for   deposits

The Serpent's Rattle

Can little girls become strong women
After knowing they are a product of adultery
Inheriting the story of love,
Child from both predator and victim

Do you know how little girls can become good women
When they are taught to live for a man
To give what they have not yet received – loyalty

Do you know how to teach little girls to become confident women
When they are ashamed of their homes
Of their parents
Of their beginnings

Do you know how little girls can grow up with honor
When their own fathers erect at the thought of penetrating them

Do you know how little girls can learn to trust a man when she can't even trust her image

-do you know how to tell the mirror 'I'm worthy' when everything inside of you was created in sin

Little boy I've heard your cries
I've come to save you from the chastised.
Come, sit on this grown woman's lap.
Do you feel safe

Bathe your tongue in my fresh water;
Find your freedom again.
Once you've located it,
Promise me you'll grow up straight.

-serpents wear skirts too

While I wish to understand what happened to you
I know it's not a strong code
To share another man's conquest

It is not my intention to know what it's like
Having your home invaded
Through the sliding doors leading to the yard

So let's not try to pretend that you and I are the same
Simply because little boys and girls
Are raped everyday

The Serpent's Rattle

All I want to say,
As a mother, I'm sorry.
I wasn't there to save you.
I'm sorry I failed you.
I'm sorry for dying in the wandering;
Forgetting you required strength.
This is not part of the script of becoming a man.

If I was your mother this is where I would begin

-a mother's apology to every boy who's been raped and couldn't say the serpent's name because he was a boy

Little boys, I know you have been hurt too.
I know serpents haunt you.

I know your ego bruised when she called you foul Names.
I know you can't share the story of the uncle that invaded your space.

Little boys I know how difficult this agony feels.
I know you feel hopeless when your fathers
Hurt your mothers
Beats on you next.

I want you to know,
Little boy,
I still believe in you.
Just don't follow snakes into their cage.

The poison will take over you,
Hypnotize you into taking over the serpent's reign.

-the passing of serpent's fangs

Salvation tides are rising
Send our rivers to wash away these sins
Summon redemption to transcend this poison
Into a formula of self-care

If you can hear me,
If you can see me,
Kneeling in the center pews of Roman Catholic suffocation
Of hope and rage
Please tell Satan to leash his pet

Tell him to stop tainting us in self-pity
Please, I beg you.
As my faith dwindles
And I begin to accept
I'm the sacrifice mother asked you to take.
A plea bargain she made,
For learning to live in the consequence of the long line of our Latina women's descent.
The greatest payment for the sin of nursing serpent venom.

-the inheritance of the loving comfort of self-hate (final prayer)

Astrid Ferguson

rESIDUAL effects

The Beautiful Story of Mayhem

Serpent's venom enters your veins, spreads like a disease throughout your body. Constricting your lungs so you suffocate on hate. The disease manifests itself into cancer in your chest so you become stone cold. An ice box without any emotions of self-worth. What many don't seem to understand is that it doesn't stop spreading. It begins to look for a new host.

I remember saying, " Leave him momma, he only causes you pain; Momma he watches me bathe." Her response and actions were as if she didn't care about my safety. She was so numb by this infection called love that she forgot to fight for our lives.

The only two sentences that I heard were, "Mind your own business and I will fix this." A day later she was in his bed, laughing, going about a normal day, while he was looking for his new host. Except I had already turned to stone before he tried to bite me again.

See, that is the thing about cancer. Once it eats away at everything organic you have left, you become best friends with your new host. So I survived by hating them both equally. Something I still regret because she needed my shoulder just like I needed her hugs. That is how this disease keeps spreading. It keeps you captive in sickness with no cure to erase all its harmful thoughts.

Astrid Ferguson

Why couldn't she be more like:
Rosa Parks / Harriet Tubman / Ida B. Wells / Correta Scott King /
Celia Cruz / Dolores Huerta / Gloria Estefan

Why couldn't she erase our stories
Create a new narrative for us all
Just like all these women who changed history

Why couldn't she just stand up and leave

I guess I forgot
It was between her legs where he bit off her soul

-a child's interpretation of abandonment

The Serpent's Rattle

I am not a survivor
So don't try to convince me
I am a caged bird who tries to sing
I am strong enough
Because in the end
I am a victim
I am an apple who didn't fall too far from the tree
So don't try to tell me I am meant to live
I have been silenced by the political debates
Of what you considered OK

Will my unborn daughters become the next prey
What do you consider keeping a woman safe
How do we convince the world to respect us
When you only use my pain for material gain
So am I really as precious as the world says

(read it upward and downward)

-I know why the caged birds sing (homage to Maya Angelou)

Astrid Ferguson

By accepting to be someone's doormat
You never get past the front door
Of a castle to occupy your seat
As a bestowed queen on her throne.

-allowing others to wipe themselves clean with you while you lay dirty in misery

The Serpent's Rattle

Sometimes I struggle with the word "Queen"
Sometimes I struggle accepting that word applies to me
Not because I don't think I'm worthy

Instead

I feel the programming taking hold, sending handwritten software into my mental one,
That I was bred to clean in between the queen's toes.
I was raised to polish the table
Where royals eat.
Cleaning the kitchen
Meant
Washing dishes,
Wiping down counters,
Sweeping, sweeping, sweeping
Everyone's mess away.
Grab a mop
No, I am sorry that is incorrect,
A hand rag, to help everyone see my broken identity
With a squeaky clean polish of *Simple Green*.

Sometimes I struggle with the word "Queen"
I look at my bank account
I look at my family
They both say by sticking together
We can make loose change into folded commodities

These are not struggles fitted for a queen
I look through so many pages and I don't see a queen that looks like me.
I am not light enough for England
I am not dark enough for Africa
I am the ongoing story of the in-between.

Sometimes I struggle with the word "Queen"
It wasn't a word my mother taught me,
It wasn't an even exchange between my siblings.
It's a word that was never hummed around the house
On cool summer days.
This positive reinforcement before beatings and shame
Is a new thing, a modern day twist.

The lectures always included,
simply do as you're told and *sit quietly*
Follow instructions without asking for clarity;
All things unsettling for a queen.

Sometimes I struggle with the word "Queen"
But I am getting used to *reina*
Negra, amor, love
After-all, my father did name me after a German princess.

Why would he hand me such monarchy
If he didn't believe in my reign

-sometimes I struggle with the word queen because I am still harvesting my crown

God isn't listening
He's preparing you for the world
God isn't listening
He's putting you through war
So you can win the battle
God isn't listening
Your prayers are being stored
While the serpent tells you they're unheard
God isn't listening
Believe in his timing
God isn't listening
G O D   A R E   Y OU   T H E R E
Welcome to the life of Jesus
The definition of pain and suffering

If he didn't save his only son from
Our damnation of sins,
Why would you think
He would save you
From the serpent's pin

-when unanswered prayers are answered with an unexpected huge responsibility

The Serpent's Rattle

You're not good enough
Thunders the lightning.
You're not brave enough
Powders the clouds.
You're not skinny enough
Howls the wind.
You're not young enough
Shimmy the trees.
You're just not appealing enough for us to water your reign.

Stay strong, your babies need you.
Stay strong, the world needs you.
Stay strong, you need you.
Stay strong, you're much stronger than them
They just can't see past their own dismay
Trickles the rain

-thunder versus rain in the quiet storm

Little girls' cries sound like⋯
Pure desperation
Infused with organic disbelief
An unwavering howl for protection.

Women's cries sound like⋯
Tricking rain on a dreary day:
It's slow at first, but remains steady
Becoming a storm thundering for change
A loss of strength with every drip of convenience
A whistling bird cry
Whose flown the wrong way and can't
S t e e r right.

The difference between a little girl and a woman's cry
One will reach for a tissue and save herself
While the other, still learns what saving means.

When a little girl finally understands the woman she is meant to be
She will reach for the sand paper,
Sand away every scar
Until it's smooths enough to hide.
Raise her middle finger
And fuck every right and wrong
Scripture *sus padres le enseñó*.

The Serpent's Rattle

-little girls grow from scars like crooked flowers in the rain

Astrid Ferguson

She's tired of
        Feeling

She wants to become light
Breathe a little softer
Work a little less
At
Worrying about
Everything

She's tired of
        Feeling

Humanly
Incapable of
drying out emotions, and
growing in vines of inadequacy

Recipe of My Own Reckoning

I. Handful of salt water on my paper cut fingers from every unsaid word in my head that dies in dusty notebooks.
II. ½ cup of sugar so I can sugarcoat the rage of feeling replaceable.
III. 1 cup of buttermilk so I can appear light and fluffy when I'm done baking up false responses to how I really feel.
IV. 2 cups of flour to white bleach my thoughts into suppressed flurries that live in halls. Mix in all recipes of this continuous I'm not good enough, cyclical delusion.
V. Butter the round cake, add the lemon zest so all the combusted emotion can rise in a perfectly round pound cake.

Astrid Ferguson

I'm confident enough in my determination
But I'm humble enough
To know
I still give up.
H O P E.

The Serpent's Rattle

Are you fragile or are you soft
Will you break instantly when dominance raises its claws
Will you bend when serpents slither on your lawn
Blending in grass
Absorbing the fertilizer and drying your soil

Are you fragile or are you soft
Will you allow the Lupus infected pins on walls, fall
Pierce through your foot callus
Deteriorate your muscles
And strangle your esophagus

Are you fragile or are you soft
Will you give the serpent your children as a sacrificial offering
Are you willing to become the chaotic recycled waste
Monster's toss in sewers
Only to be picked apart like leftovers
On hopeless dinnerplates

Fragile, you'll break into a million pieces
Which everyone else will duct tape into their own craftmanship
Soft_ you bend but you don't break
So which one will you be when the serpent picks you next?

-the constant battle of having to choose between how not to break instead of resisting abuse

Astrid Ferguson

Pain has a way of lingering
It flutters around like debris
After high fumes
Forming black scars of smoke
Even when you rinse it with growth
You can still taste the burnt photos stuck in your throat

-standing on a ledge thinking of diving into hope

Amazingly enough
We assign
People and institutions
Fire extinguisher roles
For the wild fires we create
In our own home

-playing both victim and criminal of our self-destruction

Seeing the sun in the morning,
Serves me memoirs of warm giggles.
Seeing the moon at night,
Serves me gratitude of white solace.

Everything in between covers like
White egg shells.
A protection of the masked
Ethics checked in squares
Remaining a mystery because I don't hang around for common interpretations.

The unseen perceptions that distinguish
Right from wrong
Where my right can be your wrong
Your wrong can be my right.

There's no distinction
No competition,
It's just the faith; we can
Climb the same mountains
Using different cords.

Instead, you decided to treat me like the horizon
Saying there is no right or wrong.
Overbearing my thoughts with your ideas:
Dark religion

No meaning,
No hope
No respect
For the essence of my life,
My feelings,
Emotions.

See, it didn't matter that I believed in you and me; us.
To you it only mattered; Nihilism
You had no right to break down the meaning
To respect my wrongs,
Not inflicting your darkness is my right.

I'm not cracking my eggshells
To continue picking out your infection.
When the stars align,
I'm ready to accept this fullness the sun and the moon devised,

Astrid Ferguson

I will carve myself out of a quail's egg,
Make arrows out of the bones you left to rot
Shoot them straight through your flesh and decapitate your head.

-surviving the piercings of domestic abuse

Victim

The name you don't want to hear

Victim

The last checkbox you wished stayed unchecked

Victim

The last thing you want to write in a police report

Victim

The one title you never want to murmur

Victim

The last story you never wish to tell

It happened. Your home was invaded. Molestation, sexual assault, rape, abuse, a goliath of inflicted pain. Your story matters. What was done to you was wrong in so many ways. No matter how big or small you deserved to keep that smile on your face. This is not a normality no matter how many times you hear it happened to your friends. Don't allow this abnormality to make you feel normal enduring pain. Love can be gentle and kind. You are not exempt from being happy for choosing to speak up. They will ask you a million times to tell your stories. They will take a million pictures making you feel more embarrassed with each flash.

The prosecutors will come. They will twist your words. You may not even win the court case. Your predator may get away and hurt another prey, the same or worse. What matters is that you said, 'No!' The hardest word you will ever whisper. You are not a victim. You are an innocent bystander and you have the permission to say, "*I will not be anyone's puppet any longer.*" You are still the queen/king of your home. Don't give away your crown to the intruder enforcing their stay.

OVERcoming

The Serpent's Rattle

A woman dresses provocative
    She provokes sexual assault

A mother not by choice
    She's a murderer for choosing to abort

A teenager raises her voice
    She motivates the consequential abuse

A little girl grows in the silence of her mother's broken nose
    Her innocence entices a predator's choice

Every stage of womanhood she is held accountable for the irreparable damage done to her. Just like Eve has been made a fool by the serpent, it was her fault and not the serpent's for making a fool out of her.

"If you fool me once, shame on you" is not a saying that applied to us women.
Defame was and always will be the congregation's first choice.

In every article a woman who stands up for her right to say 'no', is considered:
Perished goods, bitch, another woman seeking revenge, another hag ruining a man's name.

- when do we get to call our bodies, our lives, our voices as our own

Astrid Ferguson

Women can't
rape themselves
Impregnate themselves
Or even make the same salary wage
That's why we weren't born
with dicks between our legs.

The Serpent's Rattle

Which one was your favorite fang of poison
Which one screamed louder to your cowardly ways of increasing her misery

Which one

Should she shoot first
Your penis
Or
Your hands

So you can no longer use her as your punching bag
Door mat
Psychological psychotic experiment
Garden of weeds
Tell me
    Tell me
        Tell me
Before she pulls the trigger
Crafted with *no one is afraid of you anymore*
Cut off your head and use your rattle
In her salsa dip before this last domino hand: Capicu!

- *when the poison wears off*

Astrid Ferguson

Your armor axioms,
With toxins of thin steel.
You coward like evaporated salt,
When revenge strongly reproaches.

With toxins of thin steel,
You plant rage fool-heartedly.
You coward like evaporated salt.
Leaving whips to summon insecurity.

You plant rage fool-heartedly,
Redesigning discouragement.
Leaving whips to summon insecurity.
Reeking with tyranny in chicken bones.

Redesigning discouragement,
Your armor axioms,
Reeking with tyranny in chicken bones,
When revenge strongly reproaches.

-for the oppressor (coward)

The Serpent's Rattle

The hard truth about mankind
Is that it's easier to say,
"*You won't amount to shit*"

It's less work to keep a person stuck in a nightmare
Out of their fear of being left behind
And you prevailing with your honesty

The hard truth about mankind
Is that oppression is written in every historians library
Conflict is our humanities plague.

It is at the brink of a spear,
The other side of a shotgun,
The tied loophole of a rope
The invasion of coiled hunger,
The invaded wombs of women in every color.
Both oppression and progression were founded.

So what do you think happens now

You forget what they told you
You listen to the little voice inside of you
That says,
Move on

-staying stuck in hatred only keeps them owning your freedom

I think what made me cute
As a little girl
No longer makes me
A solid woman

-timid

The Serpent's Rattle

Mothers I demand you to teach your daughters
more than just how to set tables,
cook meals,
more than folding and ironing clothes.

Teach them⋯ Teach them⋯
Domestic duties shouldn't be your primary qualification to keep a man

Teach them⋯ teach them⋯
Not to settle for a "you're beautiful" as their face value.
Taking these chipped coins as payment for unzipping their skirts
and allowing inconsistencies to fill their loins.

Teach them⋯ Teach them⋯ teach them⋯
To stomach more than just words that
Men wear like scarves
to cover their mouths beset with lies.
Teach your daughters to become strong women so they don't have to stomach weak men.

Teach them
    Teach them
        Teach them
What my mother never taught me

How to become a woman before becoming the mankind's maid.

-enrollment in being a woman first

I might be the composition of rejection
Symphonies of hard trials
Melodies of unsung superheroes
But that is the beginning of every legend

I am still a champion
Wearing pencil skirts and stockings

-I'm still a superwoman (I believe you are too)

Self-love isn't perfect
It's not like the meadows full of fall leaves
Radiating in an afternoon cool breeze

Self-love isn't perfect
It's not like an artifact with archeological tribal patterns
Resembling victories of unanimous defeat

Self-love isn't perfect
Predictable
Or dependable

It's not like catching some well needed
Shut eye when you grow sick and tired of your identity

Self-love isn't perfect
It's not a magic trick,
Nor a wizard's spell
To make everything ugly go away

Self-love isn't perfect
It's the perfectly imperfect way of accepting you are
Equal part demon and angelic
It's knowing that today you might hate everything you see
But tomorrow you'll admire everything you missed

Take your time with self-love
For self-love also requires an unwavering commitment
During the roughest hurricanes.

-perfection was never a requirement to become self-loved

The Serpent's Rattle

Love
Takes time.
Patience, committed consistency,
Where complacency can't assist.

Did I fall short of your outlined narrative
Did I surpass all your expectations and this outcome crescendos your rage

Apologies
Bending
Curating
Consistencies, a need for a possible relationship
Me constantly begging was your vision of our friendship

You want me to apologize like a hallmark card with sprinkles
And cute phrases
So you can toss me away in a pile full of perspectives
Calling my story a cliché
While standing on a pedestal you created
Plagiarizing my pain
Here's an apology never written;
I'm sorry you thought of me as a perspective friend.
An every now and then person your phone favors,
An overqualified person of color,
But too light to stand with you on the award stage.
Under qualified for perfection;
My tongue full of bad grammar and semi-colons in the wrong place.
Growing hair too curly,
Instead of long horse hair;
Just not kinky enough
For relaxers every 13th business day.
For being broken but not shattered into a million shards
Of all the demographics that make up my DNA.

I am sorry you couldn't figure out the pieces that created my puzzled image so you can pretend to care.

I've grown tired of apologizing for your mistakes;
Your denied acceptance.
This is my sincere apology for ever thinking I needed you to read my page.
I'm setting you free so you can find someone else
To place in your cocoon of plastic covers and magazine outreach.

Signed,
The boring person who never fits the ballot of having anything interesting to say.

-grown tired of never being good enough for someone else's gain (I hope you have too.)

Where was your protection
All this manhood you claim
All these wonders you profess in a King's stance
Denying us equality
Taking away our decision making abilities

Where was your protection
When I was tossed in the white, black, brown, orange
Every man's colored bed to fuck up our pure race
Where were you sitting when the Willie Lynch letters were typed in permanent ink

Where was your protection
When you worked in offices
Demanding hot meals, pressed shirts and homemade desserts
Expecting clean laundry
While you delivered infidelities

Where was you protection
When I believed in your leadership
While you blindly led us to failures and sexually transmitted diseases
Telling me you wanted a family but you enjoyed little boys booties

Where was your protection
When I said I wasn't ready
I didn't want your penetration
I couldn't bear children
I was too young and hadn't learned
To wilt and uproot
Self-love

Where was your protection
When I wasn't allowed to pick love
I was banned from the sun's acknowledgement
Because I had a monthly red crescent in my pants

Where was your protection
When I wanted a library card so I could self-educate
Courses on financial responsibility
Earn a ballot in a candidacy
A vote in your diplomacy.

Where was you protection
During the transportation home that resulted

In human trafficking
Pimps kissing me on my forbidden cheeks
While hitting me with a fist that dislocated my hips

Where was your protection
Where was your protection
Where was your protection

I've grown tired of waiting for a king to fill the roles:
Protector, lover, man
Whose ribs I fit

I'm protecting myself from this day forward
So please stop trying to understand why feminist movements exist
Stop saying it offends you

When it was under your protection that feminism began
The time of longing for your protection has expired
I can wear a skirt and pants at the same fucking time.

-your protection is no longer sought, this is for every woman who has been let down by a man she thought she could love

My heart is tired
My palms grown stiff
Exhausted of being treated like a pawn
Sacrificing myself first while you sit comfortably
Laughing in silence to see who will swallow me first
The knight, bishop or the rook
With two right hooks
I make my way
I may lose the war but I will win the game
I've reached the other side
I am crowned queen
Calculate your last move
The buzzer is raised; your time is up

-checkmate

There are more than seven billion people in the world

You are not the only survivor
You are not the only victim
You are not the only oppressor

You are not alone in
~~Needing~~ wanting help

The world is listening
Even if the justice system dissipates your voice

-for you surviving in silence

The Serpent's Rattle

You and I are compositions of rejection,
The symphonies of hard trials
Melodies of the unsung superheroes

Even in this sad composition
We're still the uncommon definition
Of the last standing champion

-ladies, we're still winning even when we're losing rounds

Astrid Ferguson

I used to be called too emotional – sensitive
I used to be signaled to hold my tongue—
permission   to   speak

I used to be teased over my name – Astrid the uncrowned princess

I used to be clowned by my choice of clothing – Knockoffs was mother's budget

I used to let all these things hinder me from playing with children
Not that I hated playing
I just knew playing ended with the echoing of their insensitive laughter

The cackling of you lose and we win every time
The boys trying to stick their heads under my uniform
Reminding me of the serpent's torture

Only to learn
That these were all sharpeners
For my number two pencil
I would trace with permanent ink
to fill the spines of books
They would one day pay to read

-*I'm stronger standing on bookshelves*

The Serpent's Rattle

I want to be remembered for being a good person
I want my life story to begin with
I helped someone today

Even if the serpent bit me and inserted his venom in my veins
I still used my teeth to keep some holy water
Hydrating my lips

- The everyday kindness bucket list (what's yours)

Astrid Ferguson

"No one can make you feel inferior
without your consent."

-Eleanor Roosevelt

Cut this out and put it in your pocketbook. Pull it out every time someone tells you your truth will affect their reputation.

It's not anyone's responsibility
To educate you on being happy.

It's not anyone's goal to motivate
Your discrete passions.

It's your choice
    Your life
        Your duty
            Finding happiness
But sometimes
    You'll meet ~~angels~~ soldiers
    along the way

-happiness is worth fighting for

Pondering what the little girl version of me
would think about me today

Wondering if she would believe the ghost of the future
travel like Scrooge to see nightmares end

I keep her in my thoughts
Fill her name in memory banks
I want her to believe
I am not the only one who will never forget
everything she didn't say.

-never lose sight of the little girl that prayed for you every night before   bed

For the hurt
For the pain
For the discomfort
For the hatred
For the insanity
For the shame
For the silence
For the oppression
For the serpent
For the unwanted
For the surviving

For the past
For the lost identity
For the hopeless
For the little girls
For the little boys
For my mom
For my family
For me

-this is the last candle I will blow while holding betrayal as our cake

You write something from your heart

They ask for more⋯

You spill your emotions like oozing liquid from holes in a cup

They ask for more⋯

You write your vulnerabilities, your grieving desires in hopes of visibility

They ask for more⋯

You write your secrets, your private thoughts until your knuckles battle the turned page

They ask for less⋯

You write so much until the blood dries a dessert

As if your emotions are a jigsaw piece, scratched out by someone else's pen.

-write what you would want to read, even if you're the only one reading it

This page is left blank so you can insert your story even if the only one advocating for you is your pen.... Don't stay silent.

aBOUT tHE aUTHOR

Astrid Ferguson, is the momma of the book *Molt*. An emerging poet, blogger, part-time writer, mother of two boys, wife to an emerging Philly artist, novice photographer, major foodie, professional dancer (in her mind), and a lover of all things creative. Astrid is an Afro-Latina (Haitian and Dominican descent) born in Dominican Republic. She migrated to the United States at the early age of one. A passion for poetry developed after Astrid dealt with childhood hardships and abuse. She has been involved in several spoken word events and has been published in several literary magazines such as: Genre Urban Arts, Harness Magazine, Visual Verse, and Literary Orphans to name a few. Astrid hopes to one day become a slam poetry winner, a more hands-on activist and become a New York Times bestselling author.

Follow her journey in the following social media outlets:
Website: www.astridferguson.com
e-mail: amarin1203@gmail.com
Instagram: astrid_ferg
Twitter: ferg_astrid
Facebook: Astrid Ferguson – Afergtale

www.ingramcontent.com/pod-product-compliance
Lightning Source LLC
Chambersburg PA
CBHW071205070526
44584CB00019B/2920